Chapter 1: The Pros and Cons of Earning a Passive Income

Money doesn't grow on trees, as you may have heard. You have to work hard to earn money. Many people work hard for money and spend most of their time working. You earn an active income if you work for an office or a company. This is income that comes from the sale of services. This includes tips and salaries.

A 9-to-5 job is exhausting and cannot be very rewarding. It is a tedious job that requires you to get up in the morning to prepare for work. You then drive to or commute to the office and then spend the rest of the day behind a desk or in a cubicle. You receive a fixed monthly salary. You do the exact same thing every day. You may feel bored from time to time, but there aren't many things you can do.

Routines can become monotonous and exhausting. Your energy may be drained. Your stress levels may be exacerbated by your boss, coworkers and workload. You can schedule a leave if you are sick, have to attend to a personal matter, or need to be absent from work due to a family emergency.

It isn't really bad to have a job. A regular income is earned, as well as insurance. You can apply to a credit card and get a loan. You can purchase the essentials you need such as food and water. Your earnings might not be sufficient to purchase the things you desire, such as a new bag or shoes or a weekend getaway.

Sometimes you may feel like your efforts are not being properly compensated. You might want to switch from an active income source to a passive one when this happens.

What Is Passive Income?

Passive income is the income that you can earn without much effort. It is not as hard to earn passive income as active income. It is closely linked to unearned income, and it is still received on an ongoing basis. It is also taxable. Passive income can be property income, rent from properties, business earnings, income that does not require direct involvement from the merchant or owner and bank account interest. Royalties, bank account income, royalties, online earnings, interest and dividends from securities such as stocks and bonds, and pensions are all examples.

Benefits of Earning a Passive Income

Earning passive income has many benefits. There are many drawbacks. These are the pros and cons to consider before you quit your job.

A passive income can be a great way to make money. You can set your own work hours and take breaks whenever you like. You can wake up whenever you want and not have to worry about being on leave from work. If you can keep your passive income streams, you can take a vacation at any time of the year.

A passive income is attractive for students, stay-at-home mothers, and people with disabilities. It is possible to work from home. You don't have to wear office clothes or follow a dress code. You no longer need to dress up for work. You can now work in your pajamas. You can wear a nice top if you need to communicate via Skype or Webcam, but still wear your bottom pajamas.

This is especially great if you have children or pets. You can both take care of your kids and make money. Your pet doesn't have to be left at home. Both can be enjoyed! If you work hard, you can make as much money in freelance as someone who works in an office. You can take on as many projects as possible if you work freelance.

Online money-making opportunities don't require any degree beyond a bachelor's. You can succeed at your job if you're able to do the job well. It is easy to meet the requirements. If you have an Internet connection and a computer, you can get started working. You may also need a land line phone for some work-from-home jobs.

However, it is easy to get started. You can often get started as soon as you sign up. Passive income is less tax-exempt than regular income. You can enjoy lower taxes if your income comes from your own business. If you have any questions about taxes, don't hesitate to ask a professional.

You don't have to worry about being fired. If you don't want to work, you can quit. Your work can be taken with you to any place, such as a coffee shop or library. Because you don't have to deal directly with people, you can enjoy peace of mind. Because of office politics, it can be quite stressful to work in an office environment.

It is far less stressful to work in a virtual office. Even if you don't like the person online, you can still work with them remotely. Online conferences allow you to meet clients. This takes less time and energy. This allows you to do more work. You will also save money on travel costs.

You don't have to do much work in the beginning to earn passive income. Your income streams will stabilize naturally. To start your business, you don't have to do everything. After that, you can relax and wait for the money. It is still necessary to maintain the property, but this is much easier.

Drawbacks of Earning a Passive Income

There is no perfect world, and passive income streams are no exception. The biggest problem freelancers have is their low income at the beginning. It usually takes time for a business establishment to become popular with consumers. It is impossible to expect to make a lot of money in a short time. It takes patience and perseverance to make a lot of money. Don't lose heart. Keep working hard and you'll soon reach your goals.

You may not like working from home if you're the type of person who does more work with others. You aren't in a traditional office environment so there is no one around. You work alone in your own private office at home. You can't chat with anyone except via the Internet. Because there are no people five feet away, you cannot have a social existence. If you're used to people being around, working at home can be very difficult. Sometimes it can be lonely.

Success isn't always guaranteed, as with everything else in life. It doesn't matter how much research you do or how long it takes to build a website that is amazing. You may still not get the results you desire. Your website, blog, or online shop may fail despite all your hard work. This should not discourage you from getting started. Even if you work a full-time job, success is not guaranteed. Even if you don't do well, it is possible to get fired.

The pros of passive income are still more appealing than the cons. This venture offers a lot of potential for success. You will discover how to make passive income by selling on Etsy, which is a well-known selling platform.

Chapter 2: All About Etsy

What Is Etsy?

Etsy, a peer-to-peer, peer-to-peer, e-commerce site, focuses on vintage, hand-made, and factory-manufactured products and supplies. They offer art, clothing and photography as well as bath and beauty products, toys and food. There may also be tools and supplies for crafting, such as wire and beads. To be considered vintage, an item must be at least 20 years old. Etsy is home to over fifty million users.

A Brief History of Etsy

A small company called iOS pace launched Etsy in April 1998. The company was comprised of Haim Shoppach and Chris Maguire. Maria Thomas and Jared Tarbell joined them later. It took over two months for the first version to be up. Kalin decided to name the website after he felt it didn't make sense, as he was trying to create the company from scratch. Actually, the name "Etsy" was derived from the Italian words "eh, it", which means "oh, yes". These words translate into Latin and French as 'what if?'.

The company gained attention in their first year due to their constant additions of new features to the website. They were able to help sellers gain traffic and exposure. Etsy had more than one million dollars in sales by May 2007. They saw a 43 percent increase in sales, with three hundred thousand items sold on Etsy in November 2007. The company was also funded by Union Square Ventures, Jim Breyer and Hubert Buda Media in January 2008.

People began to speculate that Etsy might be taking over eBay in February 2012. Some sellers expressed disappointment and dissatisfaction with Etsy's handling of complaints about their stores. The effectiveness and user-friendliness of Etsy and eBay were then compared. It was discovered that certain items were difficult to find on Etsy, and that the site's interface seemed slow. Etsy was prone to only focus on US-based consumers.

Rob Kalin handed Maria Thomas the CEO position in July 2008. Many long-standing employees, including Chris Maguire, Haim Shoppach and Haim Stronach, left the company shortly after. Former Yahoo!! employee Chad Dickerson was hired to be the new Chief Technology Officer in September 2008. Chad Dickerson, a former employee of Yahoo! Concerns had been raised about vendors selling other people's work as their own. The company addressed these concerns.

In April 2009, etsyday was created and promoted via Twitter. This attracted more attention to the company. Etsy employed 60 people and earned $10 million to $13million each month by May 2012. The recession in the United States led to a greater demand for personalized and cheaper products. This drove Etsy's sales growth.

People Search was launched in March 2011. It was a social network system similar to Facebook. It was designed to connect buyers and sellers, and allow them to communicate. This feature was not a big hit with buyers and sellers. It actually caused many complaints as it made it much easier for buyers and sellers to find past purchases with feedback.

After raising forty million dollars in Series funding, Etsy became a B Corporation in May 2012. This was to help the company expand in foreign markets like France, Australia, Germany, and Germany. Etsy permitted drop shipping and factory-manufactured products on its site in October 2013. This was subject to the seller designing the item or hiring professional designers. They must also tell Etsy about the factories they use.

Selling and Buying on Etsy

The main functions of Etsy are selling and buying. You can sell art supplies, vintage items, and handmade goods to customers if you become an Etsy seller. Etsy offers global shipping to help you ship your merchandise worldwide. Sign up to create a username. You can also select a name to use for your store. Remember that once you create your username, you cannot change it.

Etsy won't charge you to set up a store but you will have to pay $0.20 per listing. These listings will remain on your page until your customer buys your product, or for as long as four months. You, the shop owner, have the ability to set your own prices. Etsy will require you to pay 3.5% of your earnings. A bill will be sent to you detailing the fees that Etsy owes at the end each month. Your bill will be due by the 15th of each month.

You can also become a buyer. Etsy makes it easy to search for items. You just need to type the name or description of the product that you are looking for into the search bar once you get to their homepage. The homepage also has a list. You can browse through the list to see different categories, such as jewelry, vintage, craft materials, gift ideas and mobile accessories.

You might also want to check out "Categories", which has over 30 categories and sub-categories. You can shop by color, as well as search for treasuries and curated collections that have been selected by buyers or sellers. Shop local to find the hottest and most popular items in your area. You can search by name if you are looking for a specific shop or seller. Simply type the name of the shop/seller into the search bar.

You can narrow down your search results by categorizing them by price or place. To view additional information about the items, click on them. You can avoid being scammed and disappointed by your transactions by reviewing the feedback from the sellers you plan to purchase from. You can get a sense of the reliability of the store by doing some research.

It is also helpful to have recommendations or references from trusted family members, friends, and others. If you are interested in the most current and popular items on Etsy, you can subscribe to our e-mail list. Other newsletters can be subscribed to that provide news, tips, and suggestions. You can also get gift cards that you can give to your friends and family, or to use for personal shopping.

Once you have found the product you like, click "Add To Cart" to add it to your virtual shopping basket. You can click on any number of products you like and add them to your virtual shopping basket. You can pay for your items one time, so it won't be difficult to pay. To shop on Etsy, you will need an account.

You can sign in to your Facebook account if you already have one. It's much easier to connect your Etsy account and your social network account. You no longer need to fill out forms and confirm your email address.

You can modify your public profile and personal information. You can edit your account information and shipping information. You can also edit the applications you use.

Registering for an Etsy Account is completely free. There is no fee to join Etsy. Only the items you purchase are required to be paid. Upon checkout, you can see the total cost of the items and the shipping costs. So you can see exactly how much you will need to pay, the total cost of each product will be displayed.

There are many ways to pay for your purchase. PayPal, credit cards and debit cards are just a few of the payment options available. For fear of identity theft, many people hesitate to give out their financial and personal information. PayPal is a safe and secure option if you're worried about your credit card being hacked. PayPal is a secure and safe payment platform that you can use from anywhere. It is accepted by most major retailers around the world.

Chapter 3: Pros and Cons of Being an Etsy Seller

Why should you sell on Etsy

Etsy sellers have many benefits. If you are looking to make decent cash, here are some of the benefits to selling on this peer-to-peer ecommerce site.

Etsy is a trusted platform for sellers and buyers around the world.

If you want to be a seller, reputation is a key factor. Businesses and major brands do everything they can to maintain a positive reputation. It's easy to ruin a reputation or name and it can be very difficult to rebuild it. It can be difficult to restore your business to its former glory once it is gone. Etsy has a great reputation. It has been heard of by people from many industries around the globe. It's also featured in blogs, magazines, and on television. You may also be familiar with Etsy, which is the handmade version of eBay.

Etsy is user-friendly.

It is easy to navigate the site, even for people of different ages. Even if you don't have any technical knowledge, it will be easy to navigate the site. It   is easy to list items. Simply select the header, keywords and price. You can then upload images and add descriptions.

Etsy is a community.

It's more than an e-commerce site for peer-to-peer transactions. It also has a community of buyers and sellers. It allows you to communicate and interact with people from all over the country, or even around the world. You can discuss products, services, brands, etc. Talk to them about your experiences with buyers and sellers. Talking with other sellers can help determine the price and keep you up to date on the latest trends. It's a great way to share your thoughts and get feedback from others. You can also find tips and tricks for dealing with different types of buyers. You can always count on the community for help if you are stuck. You might even find new friends.

Etsy is relatively cheap.

Etsy charges lower fees than eBay. You pay $0.20 to list your item on eBay for it to last for 30 days. Your $0.20 listing can last up to four months on Etsy. This is four times the time it takes eBay. You only need to pay for the item once it is listed and then when it sells. The transaction fees charged by eBay are 3.5% more than those charged by Etsy. Selling on Etsy can be cheaper than selling on your website. Hosting and other costs can make setting up a website expensive. Etsy makes it easy to sell your first item. You don't have any previous experience selling. You might want to test whether selling handmade products is right for you. Etsy can be used as a platform to test your selling.

Etsy is interactive.

It has social buttons that allow you to select your favorite items. This is a great way to get feedback on products. Even if your products aren't yet sold, you can still receive feedback. Your products will sell more if you have more customers who comment and view your merchandise. You should therefore find ways to get potential buyers to spend more time on your page.

Etsy lets you be creative and unique.

Etsy allows you to express your creativity by selling handmade items. Don't be afraid to express your creativity and use it in your products. Making unique decors, frames and accessories can make you a lot of money. If you are a craft enthusiast, Etsy is a great place to start.

Etsy lets you sell digital products on the site.

Some online shops, like eBay, prohibit the selling or marketing of digital products. Etsy is a great place to find buyers if you are a graphic designer or just like to create digital patterns. Etsy lets sellers sell knitting patterns, sewing patterns and card images. These digital products can be emailed to customers, or they can be downloaded by giving a link. It is a great idea to sell digital products or downloadable items. This allows you to easily repeat your products without having to create or recreate them from scratch.

The Drawbacks of Selling on Etsy

Etsy, like all things, isn't perfect. There are many benefits to selling on Etsy. You should also consider its drawbacks. These drawbacks shouldn't discourage you from selling on Etsy. You should instead use your knowledge to discover ways to make these limitations work for you. You can overcome these limitations to increase your sales effectiveness.

These are just a few reasons Etsy might not be the best place to sell your items. These drawbacks come with suggestions for how to overcome them. Remember that everything is possible if you believe you can.

It can be hard to be unique on a site.

Etsy is a marketplace for handmade goods. This means you have little chance of selling the exact same item as another seller. This is a great way to show off your artistic skills and talents. It can also pose a problem. Customers may find it difficult to decide which item they want, as every seller sells unique items. Customers may look at the description of the item to learn more. Your description won't be unique if you have a great description of your product that another seller has copied. This could lead to confusion among buyers. Some buyers may mistake your shop for another.

How can you solve this problem, then? Make sure your descriptions match your products exactly. It will be impossible for another seller to copy it as it wouldn't be the same product. Don't use generic descriptions that only describe the item's size, color, or shape. If you're selling handmade dolls, don't just describe them as small, cute, or made from yarn. To make your item stand out, you must provide as much detail as possible. Make sure your words are appealing to customers. Make sure you are clear and concise with your description. However, make sure it is interesting.

It can be hard to get search engine traffic to your shop.

Google updates its algorithm regularly, so you need to be aware of this fact. However, recent updates are based upon duplicate content. If every shop sells identical merchandise with the exact same descriptions they will be penalized. Duplicate content will also result in a decrease in traffic to the site.

What can you do to stop other sellers from copying your descriptions? You can't stop other sellers copying your descriptions but you can monitor your store. You can make changes to your descriptions, but you must ensure that they only reflect what you sell. Change your product descriptions every once in a while to make them more appealing and attract more customers.

It can be hard to manage a store.

Sellers claim selling on Etsy gives them more exposure than selling directly from their websites. You can also lose customers to Etsy sellers. You can gain potential customers by allowing them to browse other Etsy stores. This can be either good or bad, but you can't have complete control over your store.

You should also consider external factors like Etsy raising the fees or you losing profit. Etsy could also ban some merchandise from being sold on their site. If they banned the type of goods you sell, it would be a big deal. You should be ready in case Etsy restricts the marketing of certain items. Etsy sellers do not have full control over their store. You will be subject to the owners as long as you're on the site. You are at the mercy of its owners, who can decide what is best for them and your store.

This problem can be solved by extensive market research. Keep up-to-date with the latest trends. Learn what customers want. You can then update your shop and offer the products that customers want. You can sell a wide range of products so that you are always prepared for any changes made by Etsy's management. You should have all the items that your customer might need. It is great to be a one-stop shop.

Chapter 4: Common Seller Mistakes and How to Avoid Them

You don't want to make the same mistakes as other sellers on Etsy if you are a new seller. Although experience is the best teacher, it is wise to do your research before making mistakes. These are the top mistakes sellers make on Etsy. We also have tips to help you avoid them.

Not having sufficient listings

This is a common mistake made by many sellers when they first begin selling. Many sellers wonder why they cannot sell any product. You are likely to see only five to ten items in their shop. Don't be like these sellers. Potential customers may think you're just a hobbyist and not a business if you only list a few products in your shop.

If you want to sell items on Etsy and make a profit, then you need enough listings. Upload at least 100 items. Do not be discouraged if you feel overwhelmed by the number of items. Keep uploading as many listings you can. Keep in mind that the more listings you have the better your business will appear in search results.

Not offering detailed descriptions

A potential sale can be made or lost if a visitor to your site comes across your shop listing. It is important to remember that you only have one chance to convince potential customers to buy your product and not to move on to the next shop.

To make a great first impression, include detailed descriptions of the product. You should tell them all they need and want about the products you sell. Give details about the dimensions, color, style and size of your products. It is important to be truthful. Be honest about the item.

You can increase their curiosity by giving them reasons to buy your products. When they make a purchase with you, tell potential customers what they will gain. Tell potential customers how your merchandise will improve their condition or help them in the long-term. Don't exaggerate when you tell them your merchandise can make a difference in their lives.

Include a personal success story if possible. If you sell adult coloring books, tell potential customers how your products can relieve tension and stress. You can tell them how much fun it would be for them to color beautiful black and white images. Encourage them to frame or hang their masterpieces on the wall.

You can convince them that their coloring books have better patterns than other ones. You can also convince them to buy your coloring books for their loved ones. Their families and friends can also start a new hobby that will help relieve stress and keep them entertained during dull days.

You should also avoid digressions. Your descriptions should be concise and to the point. One-liner descriptions are a bad idea. They are too brief. One line does not suffice to describe everything about your product. A paragraph is sufficient, provided it isn't too long. This is not an essay. You can describe the physical characteristics of your items without being too detailed.

Not maximizing the space for description

Many sellers don't make the most out of their description section. It is possible to link other sections of your shop into your description section if you are not sure. This can attract potential customers' attention and encourage them to visit your other products. It is a good idea to have a link at the bottom of your description. However, it is important to link only shop sections and not individual items. This is because the time and purchase of an item eventually ends. Their links will become "dead" as a result.

Using photos that are blurry or cluttered

You don't have a physical shop and can only rely on your virtual shop to attract customers. It is impossible to show your products in person so it is important to take great photos. Remember that photos are essential to the success of an online shop. Your potential   customers may not be able to touch, feel or smell your products but they should have the impression that you merchandise is worth their time.

To capture the essence of your product, it is important to use a quality camera. Sellers can upload up to five photos per item on Etsy. Make sure you clearly show every angle. You can still use your phone's built-in camera, even if you don't have the funds for a professional camera. However, make sure to set up lighting and find a background that will complement your items. You should arrange them so that they are attractive and presentable. Photos are still more important than words and descriptions.

Image taken from www.photl.com

Not including an About Page

Etsy offers an About Page that allows sellers to describe themselves, their business and their shop. This feature should be used to make your potential customers more interested in you. This page allows you to show off your studio and explain how your merchandise is made. Tell us about your journey to where you are today.

However, you should not only talk about your business. Don't be afraid to share something personal. People love success stories that motivate and inspire. If you want to draw more customers to your business, tell them about yourself and what your goals are. Photos of you and your business from the beginning can be included. Photos of your workplace and warehouse can be uploaded. Your About Page should be as informative as possible.

Adding unremarkable titles

Remember that the title of your merchandise can also be very important. It is the first five keywords that appear when you search for something. It could also appear in your product's HTML address. You need to choose a title carefully. It should be clear and concise. It must contain keywords that are easily included in the HTML address.

Lacking policies

Sellers are often unaware of the importance and necessity of having a policy. This is especially true if they have never worked in retail. It is important to have clear and detailed policies that address all possible scenarios. This will make it easier for potential customers to deal with you. Instead of worrying about what the future holds, and second-guessing yourself when faced with problems, it is better to simply review your policies and find a solution. A clear, concise, and detailed policy can prevent business problems.

Not using keywords or tags

Keywords or tags are essential for quickly and easily finding your products. Use words that describe your merchandise. You can spend some time brainstorming ideas. You can make sure you have considered every possible tag or keyword. Consider the material used to make the keywords and tags. It is also important to consider whether the item was popular in what era, or if it is digital. It should be described in detail, including its size, color and shape. Search engine optimization is your friend. Use it wisely.

Disregarding the shop announcement feature

Etsy lets sellers make announcements about their shops. This is a very useful feature, so be sure to use it. Adding new products to your shop will keep it current. Next, tell the public that you just added new items to your shop. Then encourage them to go check it out. To entice customers to make a business transaction with your company, you may want to use coupon codes. Promotions, discounts, and freebies are great when there's a holiday like Mother's Day, Valentine's Day or Christmas.

Not making the most of social media

Nearly everyone has a social networking account today. You can sign up for free and create an account on Facebook or Twitter. Millions of people around the world have an Internet connection and can access a computer. It is therefore easy to reach them for vintage or handmade products.

Selling on Etsy requires social media. Etsy allows sellers connect their Facebook and Twitter accounts to their shops to keep their fans and followers informed. You can also use the Pinterest pin-it buttons and other social media tools. These buttons can be used by potential customers to pin items they like to their pin boards.

Etsy already gives you an online storefront. It is up to you now to manage your marketing strategies. Social media is an effective and cost-effective way to promote your products. To keep your fans informed about the latest happenings, you can also create a fan page for your business.

You must ensure that your shop is exposed to enough people. Collaborate with bloggers to have your shop featured in their blogs and websites. You could also consider collaborating with YouTubers or people who have large followings on Instagram, Twitter, Facebook and Twitter. You can get more customers and sales if you make your shop more visible to the world.

Chapter 5: Getting Started

You now have a better understanding of Etsy's history and how to sell on the popular website. You must create a store in order to become a seller.

Sign up at Etsy's official website. After you've signed up, click "Sell" in the upper left corner. The site will redirect you to Etsy.com/Sell, where you can find out more about selling. This page will show you the categories fees, tools and support as well as stories, selling and FAQ.

Fees

Etsy claims that it is a secure and affordable platform to sell your products. The site does not charge monthly fees and automatically deposits funds to your account. At $0.20, the listing fee is very low and affordable. This is almost nothing! This is a very small sum that anyone can afford. Your listings can remain active for up to 4 months, or until they sell, depending on when it happens. After your item has been purchased, you will be charged a commission and a PayPal payment processing fee.

Tools

This is good news for all sellers. You can now spend more time improving and managing your store. No matter your level of experience, there are tools that can help you. No matter your level of selling experience, you will find the right tools to meet your needs.

You can update your merchandise, reply to customers or manage your orders from anywhere you are. The app is very useful because you don't have to be at the computer all day. You can track your store and sales wherever you are.

Tools can be used to promote your listings and attract more customers. You can also share your merchandise via social media platforms if you're on social media.

Analytics can be used to improve your sales. You can find detailed statistics showing traffic sources and performance trends to help you keep track of your business.

PayPal makes it easier to pay your bills. PayPal is accessible both locally and internationally, as you already know. Customers all around the globe can easily and securely pay you using their PayPal accounts. These accounts can be linked with their savings and credit cards.

Support

Contact their customer service if you have any questions. No matter how big or small your Etsy store, they will help you solve your problem. The support team can be reached via email or by phone.

To receive new insights and tips that will help you improve your store, sign up for the newsletter. You can also access their Seller Handbook. It is kept up-to-date by Etsy so that you can keep learning new techniques and practices for your business.

You can also interact with other sellers by joining the forums. Ask questions and get answers. Etsy is a community that helps one another succeed.

Stories

It is hard to find a positive success story about an Etsy seller. These stories will motivate and inspire you to become a better seller and reach greater success. Many of these sellers began small, just as you. Their hobbies turned into profitable business ventures. If you are persistent and give your customers what they need and want, you can do the same as them.

Selling

There is the big question: "What can I sell on Etsy?" Before you can become a seller, it is important to understand your customers. What is it that makes them curious and bored? What is it that makes them want more?

You will need to compromise, however, because you aren't selling on your website.

First, only sell what is allowed to be sold. Etsy allows you to sell handmade items, crafts supplies, and vintage goods that are less than twenty years old. You may sell your items somewhere else if they don't fall within these categories.

Frequently Asked Questions (FAQ)

You may be new to selling and have many questions. The FAQ page contains the most frequently asked questions and answers by sellers. These are just a few of the questions you might be asking.

What are Etsy's fees?

You will see in the book that Etsy doesn't charge any fees to join the community. Sign up for Etsy without paying a penny. Although joining Etsy is free and you can set up a store, selling on the site will cost you. You will still need to pay for listings, transactions and payment processing.

However, it isn't expensive to do this. You can publish your listing for $0.20 and it will stay up on the site for up four months. The listing is removed when it expires or when a customer buys the item. A basic transaction fee of 3.5% is required to sell an item. This fee does not include shipping costs.

You must also comply with PayPal's payment processing fees if you use PayPal as your primary method of payment. Etsy charges listing fees in the US Dollar. If you use another currency, the fees may be different depending on how much you pay.

What are the steps to start a shop?

It's easy to set up an account and open a store. It's easy to select a currency and store location. You will also have no trouble choosing a store name, listing your products, and setting up your payment method. You should also set Etsy's billing method and the way you want to pay your fees.

How can I get paid?

This is the most important question any seller should ask. You can state in your account that PayPal payments are accepted. The funds will then be deposited directly to your account. Although you can use your personal account to pay, Etsy recommends that business sellers open a business account. You can manage your finances much more easily. Your personal account can only receive a certain amount of money per month. Customers whose credit cards are used to fund their accounts will not be allowed to pay you.

To open a shop, do I need a debit or credit card?

If you are looking to open an Etsy store, you don't need a debit or credit card. To be approved and make Etsy a legitimate seller, you must register with your PayPal account or credit-card. You won't be charged any fees until you publish your listings or open up your store.

Chapter 6: How to Select a Name for Your Shop

Names are an important aspect of any shop or store. Your business' first impressions are crucial. Customers will either choose to visit your shop or not if they see the name. You need to pick a name that is easy to remember and will bring in as many customers possible. This name will make your shop stand out in search results, be easily searched, and be easy to remember. Here are some tips to help you choose the perfect name for your shop.

Show originality.

Although you can always draw inspiration from others, it is important to not be a copycat. Remember that being original is the key to a successful business. You must sell original and unique items if you want to become a successful seller. You must also have a unique name for your shop. Names that are visual and involve physical objects should be chosen. These names can increase your business' popularity and help you form a stronger memory. You can also use words and phrases that have a particular meaning for you, which can spark the curiosity of potential customers.

Showcase your personality and style.

Choose a name for your store that is suited to the personality and style of the seller. If you sell quirky and fun items, your store name should be appropriate. You should choose a name that is classic and elegant if you sell them. When naming your store, don't be afraid to use your imagination. You want your customers to associate your store with your products.

Try to reflect what you are selling.

You can choose a name that includes specific items if you want people to be able to find you store easily. If you sell personalized coasters, make sure you include the word "coaster" in your store name. Customers searching for coasters will be immediately drawn to your store's name and likely to visit it. However, this comes with a downside. If you want to increase your merchandise selection, it may be difficult to find customers. This is especially true if your customers are already familiar with the coasters.

Be mindful of your spelling.

You should choose a name that is simple to spell and pronounce. Although it is advisable to choose a unique and original name, customers shouldn't be confused by unusual words or special characters. You should use traditional words and correct spellings as much as possible. Potential customers won't have to remember the name of your shop and type it in the search bar. Customers might misspell your shop name and be directed to another one if it is too difficult to spell. This can lead to customers being lost. It is a bad sign for your business if you have fewer customers.

Keep it simple and short.

Avoid using a long name for your shop. It can be hard to remember and can be tedious to type. It is important to keep the shop's name short and to the point. Do not use more than three words.

Capitalize multiple words.

If your name is made up of multiple words, capitalize the first letter. It will make it easier for others to read your shop's name. The distinction is made by capitalizing the first letters. This makes it easier for you to distinguish between the words. For example, if you are selling colorful ceramic plates, you can use ColorfulCeramicPlates as the name of your shop. This is much easier to read and understand than colorfulceramicplates. Don't worry about capitalizing letters becoming a problem for potential customers when they type the shop name in the search bar. It creates visual separation. It has no effect on search results. Even if your customers use lowercase letters, they will still be able find you shop.

Take a memory test.

You don't have to visit a testing center in order to take the test. It can be done at home. It's actually quite simple. Use a piece paper and a pen to remember the Etsy shops that caught your attention. Note the names of these shops. It doesn't matter if you like the products sold in this shop. You just need to remember the names of the shops. Take a look at the names and see if there is anything you can identify. Find out what makes these names memorable and catchy.

These can then be used as inspiration to name your shop.

Use the search engines.

Google, Bing and Yahoo are all options. Enter your desired name, and hit the Enter key. What page do you see in the search results? Are you confident that you can reach the top of the search result page? It may not be a good idea if there are many shops, blogs, and websites with the same name to add to the mix. You will be difficult to distinguish yourself if you do. Your shop will be just another name.

Avoid offensive names or words.

Etsy prohibits the use of profane and racist words. You need to be careful about what words you choose. It can be frustrating and difficult to open a shop just because it has a name. It can be hard to redirect people to your shop if you already have a following. It will be exhausting to transfer your items. Even worse, you won't be able to transfer any of your sales records, feedback, or other interactions to the new shop.

Be careful with the law.

You don't want to be sued for the name of your Etsy shop. Before you decide on the name of your Etsy shop, make sure you adhere to the laws in your country and state. Some names and words are already trademarked. They are therefore not allowed to be used. Check with your Secretary to verify that a name is registered. You can also visit the United States Patent and Trademark Office site. You can also consult an attorney to get specialized advice.

Chapter 7: How to Build Branding

If you want your business success, branding is essential. You must offer high quality products and exceptional customer service. All these things are pointless if customers don't know who you are or what your shop stands for. You've probably noticed brands that appear to be of low quality but are very expensive. Celebrities and socialites love their products, as do wealthy people. Their name is what makes them trendy and expensive.

You might try a thrift shop or a smaller boutique that is less well-known. Check the price of a basic blouse or tee and get it checked out. Next, find a store that sells it at a higher price. Take a look at the price tag. It will surprise you at the similarities between the products, but the price tags are vastly different. Marketing is a major factor in this. Marketing is the key to gaining more exposure for a brand that is more expensive. You might see a celebrity endorse it. You may see it on billboards and ads all over the place.

These marketing strategies all cost money. That's why it is more expensive. It is also more appealing to the masses because it is more visible. People have a tendency to believe that what they see on television and on billboards is good. They associate items sold by the most popular brand with superior quality, even though they may be identical. They may look and feel identical, or even be made from the same material.

Your branding is essential if you want your business success and to gain a large following. Publicize your business to the world. Everybody must know about your shop and the items you sell. You must make a good first impression. Attract potential customers and convince them to stay.

What Is a Brand?

What is a brand exactly? What is a brand? Is it just a logo and a tagline. A brand is much more than that. A brand is more than a name. It is a belief and a perception. It is about creating and communicating this perception. Brand image is formed by the use of mascots and jingles. However, they are there to help create this perception.

Your brand should let people know what they can expect from you. They should know who you are and what your brand stands for. It is important to tell them what they can expect from working with you. You can attract new customers by building a strong brand and keep existing customers loyal.

How to Define Your Brand

It is tempting to focus only on choosing a name or a motif for your shop. It is tempting to only think about the colors, fonts and photos on your shop's website. These elements are a reflection of your brand's essence. Before you can decide which photos and themes to use, you need to understand what your brand's essence is. These questions will help you determine the essence of your brand.

What is your primary purpose or goal in creating and/or selling your products?

What is the purpose of this? What are you hoping to accomplish by doing this? Consider how your story aligns with the brand you want to portray to others. Remember that Etsy is a community that focuses on the authenticity and personal side of shops. Your personal story can make a big impact on potential customers and greatly affect your chances of selling. You need to tell a story that makes your customers feel special, and that their purchase of your products will increase their value. Your story should also be inspiring so they feel comfortable buying your products and giving them as gifts.

What are the most important things about your items? What makes them different from other items on the site?

Also, it is important to determine what your unique selling proposition and what your product brings to the table. Your unique selling proposition basically describes your products and their value to customers. Look at the uniqueness of your products and think about what makes them stand out. If you sell handmade mittens, consider how they differ from other handmade mittens on Etsy. You might use a particular yarn or create custom designs. No matter what reason, it is important to acknowledge it and learn about it. You must also consider your customers when selling. You can then determine what you can offer them.

What words would be the best for describing your products?

You have many words to describe the products you sell. It is up to you to choose the most appropriate words for your merchandise. If you provide photography services for dogs then you will need to choose twenty words that sum up your brand. Reduce this list until you have ten. Keep reducing your descriptions to four words. This is the main purpose of this exercise: to allow you to come up with adjectives to help you distinguish yourself from your competitors. You can also describe yourself as being soulful, playful and spiritual if your competitors are described as elegant, sophisticated, and sophisticated.

Who are your customers?

Although it's every seller's goal to have all customers, this is not possible. It is impossible to please everyone and it would be extremely difficult to meet all their needs. It is important to target a particular group or audience. Once you have identified your target audience, you can begin to build your brand to appeal to them. Find out their characteristics by doing research. Do they have a range of interests, age, or location? Try to imagine yourself as they do.

Begin to Build Your Brand

Once you have established the essence of your brand including its story and values, it is now time to determine the perception that your customers will have. When crafting your brand message, there are seven things you should remember:

1. Clear. Clear and concise is the best way to stand out from your competition and be recognized by more customers. Don't try to please everyone. It is impossible to please everyone. It is best to choose one demographic and make it great.
2. Consistent and
3. Cohesive. Make sure your brand messaging is consistent across all platforms. If your shop is glamour-oriented and your products are elegant, your flyers, emails, social media accounts, posters and business cards should reflect that.
4. Communicate. Communicate. This includes your logo, name, colors, font styles, and theme. Your brand's core attributes should be reflected in everything you do.
5. Competitor. You need to know your competitors in order to position your brand in a competitive environment. You should do some research about your competitors to find out their strengths and weaknesses. It is important to remember that positioning does not refer to your product, but to your customers. Your potential customers' perceptions of you and your position are key. Find out what other people think about the products you sell. What products do they have that you don't think they need? Which new problems do they have that you believe you can solve? What new ways do they think you can make their lives better and easier? What do you think can you do to fill the gap by serving customers that other sellers cannot? How do you think that you can solve their problems that other sellers cannot?
6. Customers. A business is just like life. It requires relationships. You must build relationships with your customers if you want to build your brand. Know your customers. This includes what they need and want. You should also find out how to deliver these items. Remember that social media marketing is the best kind of marketing strategy. This is because people will do it for you. To encourage feedback

from customers, you can use your About Page. You can also use multiple social media platforms to reach more people.

7. Attract attention. Be bold, unexpected, helpful, authentic, and memorable. People will quickly forget about you if they don't. It is not good for any company to be forgotten. You must be known if you want to build a reputation and make money. It is difficult to get the attention of customers and be recognized by them, especially when there are so many other shops. You need strategies to ensure you stay ahead of the game.

Chapter 8: How to Upload Good Photos of Your Items

As you've seen, photos are crucial for selling on Etsy. You must provide great visual aids for customers who don't have access to a physical shop where they can view your products. Although photos may not be as accurate as the real thing, they are close. You should do your best to upload high-quality photos. These photos will allow potential customers to see how your products look and feel.

Helpful Tips on Uploading Photos on Etsy

These are some tips that will help you upload photos to your Etsy shop.

Use a high quality camera.

You should make sure you use high-quality cameras to get high-quality photos. There are many digital cameras to choose from. Before you make your final decision, be sure to check reviews and review their specifications. You can still use your smartphone even if you don't have the money for a high-end camera. Don't worry, there are many techniques that you can use to improve your photos even if your smartphone is not an expensive one. These techniques will be covered in the book.

Use the macro settings of your camera for close-up shots.

The majority of items on the site can be used for macro settings. This setting is usually represented by a tulip or flower icon. However, you don't have to stick with one setting. You can experiment with many settings until you find the one that suits you best.

Try out different combinations to see if you like them.

Do not use flash.

A lot of sellers make the error of using flash with their cameras. Notice

Compare the photos you took with your flash on and the photos you took with it off. The photos that are taken without the flash will look much better. The flash bounces light off of the subject, making it look ugly. You want your photos to appear brighter so choose a location with bright but diffused lighting. Outdoor photography is great because of the natural lighting.

Image taken from www.androidauthority.com

opt for natural lighting.

Outdoor lighting is best for taking photos. You should avoid direct sunlight. This can cause your photos to be poor quality. You should instead take photos in indirect sunlight. You can choose to take photos under shade or in a place that is not directly exposed to the sun. For instance, you can remain on the patio.

◢ Take advantage of props.

Amazing photos can be created by using props alongside your items. Props can be purchased from specialty stores or found in your home. You can also use flowers to give your items a more sophisticated and elegant look. To accompany baby's clothing, you can also use small toys. To make the photos more interesting, you can add books, balloons, or other items. For handmade soap or shampoo, herbs make great props. A mannequin can be used to make hats or pieces of clothing. You can also use your body as a model if you don't have any props. Aprons look better when worn on you than on a background of solid colors. Wrapping a scarf around your neck is better than just lying on the ground. Your potential customers will be able to see the results of your products by trying them on. However, be careful not to overdo it. Remember that the item must be the main focal point of the photos. Not the props. Even if you have attractive props, the items that make the most impact should be your focal point.

Image taken from hubpages.com

◢ Use a background that can make your item pop out.

Backgrounds are key to good photos. You can use printed backgrounds or patterns if you don't have props. Be sure the background isn't too busy. A plain background is also possible. While you can pick any color, black and white are the best. White background works well with almost everything except white items. A black background, on the other hand, works well with white, gold and silver items, as well as neon-colored ones. Contrast is important here. A darker background is best for items that are pastel or light in color. Contrastively, you should choose a lighter background if your items have dark colors.

Take shots from different angles.

Make sure you take photos from all angles so your customers can see the item in different perspectives. You can take a few photos from each angle, and then you will sort them later to find the best. Sellers can upload up to five photos to an Etsy listing. Make sure you only upload the photos you require. A photo should show how the item looks from different perspectives. Upload both close-up and full-size photos. Customers will be able to see all details.

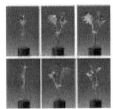

Image taken from www.shortcourses.com

Edit your images using a photo editor.

Edit means to improve the appearance of your items, not completely change their appearance. The photos should show the exact same item. Don't trick potential customers into believing that your items look different. To improve the quality of your photos, you can upload them to a photo editor after you have taken them. Photo editors can make photos look professional and help to improve their quality. You can adjust the contrast or remove background noise. Your photos may also be given a copyright watermark. You can make sure that no one else steals or uses your photos for their own purposes. You can allow others to use your photos as reference but only if they ask for permission. We will discuss photo editing in the next chapter.

Image taken from play.google.com

How to Avoid Experiencing Problems When Uploading Listing Images

Sellers sometimes experience problems uploading their images. Upload images with a resolution of 1000 pixels to avoid similar issues. You are more likely to take a large image with a digital camera. You may need to use photo editing software to resize the images before uploading them to the website.

Also, ensure that your browser is compatible with Etsy. Uploading photos can be difficult if you are using an older browser or one that doesn't support the site. Internet Explorer users should disable add-ons and toolbars that were not included with the browser.

Images should not exceed 300k in size. Uploading images with larger files can cause problems, especially if you don't have an Internet connection.

Remember that Etsy supports only files saved as.pang or.jpg and.gif. It doesn't support animated.gif files.

You should also convert your photos to RGB before uploading them. You can be sure that the colors you upload to Etsy will match your originals.

Make sure to verify your firewall settings. You have the option to modify or delete your firewall settings. You should also note that all photos listed on the site are automatically rotated. Uploading photos shouldn't be difficult. However, it may depend on what information you have in your image file.

If your listing image uploads sideways, you may use a photo editing program to rotate it. If you are holding your camera in a different place, you can also take another picture. Remember that your camera's orientation and the item you are using must match.

Chapter 9: Tips on Editing Your Photos

As you have seen, Etsy allows you to upload photos of your items. A photo editing program is one way to do this. Although you can find free online photo editors, it is better to purchase your own software. You can use all the features of the software and have it available at all times. Many free online editors or trial software programs only offer limited features, or are restricted in their availability. You can edit your photos whenever you want with your own photo editor.

It is well-known that good photos on Etsy can increase your chances to sell and attract more customers. The way you present your products can reflect their quality. Your presentation is basically your product. Customers will be more inclined to believe that your products are good if you present them well. Conversely, customers might think that your products aren't as good if they don't like your presentation.

To be able take great photos, you don't need to be an expert photographer. You can create stunning photos with the help of photo editing software programs. Photoshop is the most widely used photo editing software. It can be difficult to learn how to use. You may not be able to learn Photoshop and then open your Etsy shop. A Web application allows you to edit and upload photos immediately.

Be Funky allows users to upload photos and make necessary adjustments before downloading them again. You don't need to install any software. Online editing is possible. You don't need to share any of your information or photos online. The best part is that the Web application comes at no cost. It is free to use and you don't have to pay anything. Simply go to the official site and upload your picture.

However, there are also some downsides to using a Web app. You won't be able edit your photos if there is no Internet connection. If you have a photo editor program installed on your computer you can quickly and easily edit your photos, then upload them later when you have an Internet connection. You can save a lot of time by not having to wait or waste time when the Internet is down.

What can you do to improve your photos? There are many technical improvements you can make to your photos. You don't necessarily have to put in a lot of effort. You can simply improve the quality of your images as an Etsy seller. It is not a good idea to try to change their appearances to make them look different. These are some things that you can do to enhance your photos.

Highlights and shadows can be increased or decreased

You must make the areas that should be whiter when you highlight an item. If you didn't use enough lighting during the shoot, white areas may look grey. If you have a white background, this is more likely to happen. To fix this problem, choose Highlights and Shadows in the settings. Increase Highlights to 1.5 or 1.6. This value can change depending on how high-quality your uploaded photo is. These values can be adjusted to your liking. Make the necessary changes.

You need to darken areas that are supposed be darker when you increase the shadows on an item. Sometimes, a black item can appear greyish or grayish in a photograph. If you didn't use enough lighting, this is a common problem. To fix this issue, increase Shadows to 0.15 or any other value that is needed to get the desired result.

Increase or Decrease Saturation

You can improve the color of an item by increasing its saturation. The more saturated a color is, the more vibrant it will be. Colors become more intense if they are saturated. You should limit your Saturation to six points. You should not increase the saturation beyond six points as it can cause color burns. These colors can appear too intense and fake if they do. You can also reduce the saturation if the colors are too intense for your customers or you. You can also reduce saturation to make a color image black and white.

Crop

You can choose to crop certain areas of your image so that they are not displayed when you upload it. Zoom in on your photo, and remove any parts that are not appealing to you. Images should be cropped in square format. Images are best viewed in squares. Select Crop and then Square. Drag and click on the corners to make edits.

Image taken from
sheknows.com

Original Cropped

Straighten

You can adjust the orientation of your photo to make it appear vertically or horizontally straighter. Move the cursor across the image until the lines of grid are parallel. Depending on your needs, you can move it left or right. Remember that the larger your image appears, the more straighten it. Because parts of your image have been cut to preserve its rectangular shape, this is what happens.

After you're satisfied with the changes you made to your photos, save them. Either save them first on your computer and then upload them to Etsy later, or click Save and Share to upload the photo directly to Etsy. You may choose to save your photo in.jpg format. Make sure to set the quality to maximum. You can then save your photo the best possible way.

Chapter 10: Tips on Writing Product Descriptions

It is crucial to describe your product well and help customers understand your products. This can help them make a purchase. If you use the right words, potential customers will be more likely to add your products to their shopping cart.

Your product descriptions might not be very exciting if you are just starting to sell on Etsy. You will learn to write good product descriptions over time. These are the general rules that you should follow if you want your site to succeed.

Make an inverted pyramid.

Your most important information should be the first thing people see in your description. This will allow potential customers to quickly learn about your item. This description can be used to give potential customers more information and optimize how it appears in search results. You can use words you've used before for the title of your item.

Speak in the first person.

You can connect with potential customers by speaking in the first person. This strategy is highly effective because people are more inclined to connect with others on an individual level. Instead of being a salesperson to customers, show your personality. Think of product descriptions as a way to meet new friends. You want to be natural but polite.

Use bullet points and short paragraphs.

It is possible that people browsing your shop are looking for a particular material or size. To make it easier for them to find the information they are looking for, use bullet points and brief paragraphs. Avoid using unnecessary words or phrases that don't make sense. It is important to communicate clearly to your potential customers and to get straight to the point.

Monitor the statistics of your shop.

Make a list of keywords most frequently used by your customers. This list can be used to remind you of the most searched keywords and key phrases. These lists can be used as a guideline when creating tags and titles for your listings. Also, ensure that these key phrases and keywords are included in your descriptions. Search engines will be able to find your shop much more easily if you do this. External websites are more likely to pick up key phrases and keywords in product descriptions than they are in tags.

Include links in your descriptions.

You can include URLs in your descriptions. These links will function as hyperlinks when you do this. Links are a great idea because they grab the attention of people browsing your shop. A customer might click on a link if he sees it. If he clicks on the link, he will be taken to another section of your shop. He might make a purchase if he likes what they see. Links in product descriptions are useful because they don't allow customers to get away with their purchases as fast. If your product description does not convince potential customers to buy, the links can redirect them elsewhere in your shop. You may redirect them to you About Page, where they can read about your life, dreams, and plans. Potential customers may feel encouraged to do business with you if they have made a connection with you and learned more about your shop.

Edit your product descriptions.

Online users are more likely to become bored quickly. They are often very short-attention span people. Long descriptions can bore them and cause them to skip to the next page. You want to leave a lasting impression on potential customers by keeping your descriptions short, to-the-point, and entertaining. To connect with people deeper, you can use short and sweet prose. Make sure your descriptions are correct in grammar and spelling. If you don't have a proofreader, you can use a spelling checking software program to correct grammar and spelling mistakes.

Find your voice.

It is your writing voice which creates the unique style and personality of your shop. Your target audience is key to your voice development. Think about what message you want to communicate to them. What type of lifestyle are they living? Do your customers mostly consist of young mothers or teenagers who love to sport the hottest accessories? If your target audience is mostly women looking for gifts for their husbands, boyfriends, or soon-to-be married men, you can adjust your product listings accordingly. Men's clothing, watches and perfume can be sold, as well as other personal items.

Think physical.

It is helpful to have detailed descriptions when comparing online shopping with physical store shopping. Think about what information buyers would want if they were buying online. It is not helpful to rely on only numerical measurements. This is especially true when shopping for jewelry. Most customers don't have the ability of measuring by eye. If they don't have a ruler, which is unlikely, customers may not be able simply to eyeball 1.5 inches. To help them, you will need to provide physical reference. When describing sizes, you can use terms like "below the collarbone", or "chin length". Don't forget to include specific measurements and other technical information in the details.

Be mobile-friendly.

It is quite common to connect to the Internet with your smartphone in this age and age. Most people are always on the move. People don't have the time to sit down and use their laptops. They cannot afford to spend hours at their computers. Modern technology has enabled the introduction of smartphones, tablets, and mobile phones. You can connect quickly to the Internet from anywhere you are, whether you're walking, on a train or waiting in line. No matter where you may be, you can easily answer your emails and check the status of your social media accounts. You can also video call without any restrictions. You can access the internet as long as your mobile data is available or you are within Wi-Fi range. This means that you can expect most people to use their phones to visit Etsy. It has been shown that mobile devices account for more than half of all traffic to the site. These small screens have a lot more power than you might think. Mobile devices are a great way to get more customers' attention. You should be able write concise and memorable descriptions. Make sure you include the most important information at the top of your listings to attract more people and make Etsy more search-friendly.

Questions Your Descriptions on Etsy Should Be Able to Answer

Apart from the above tips, you should also be able provide solutions and answers to customers' most frequent questions. Remember that many of these customers are not able to touch, feel, or even try your products. You must give the information to them as if they were your eyes, ears, nose and skin.

Potential customers will be more likely to click on "add to basket" if the descriptions of your products make an impression. In other words, product descriptions are critical to a sale. Here are some common questions customers ask you to help you prepare:

What makes your products special and unique?

The product descriptions should tell a story. The story should be compelling enough to persuade others to buy from you again. However, such stories don't have to be lengthy. However, it should be long enough for potential customers to see your product. Take soda ads as an example. You may have seen an advertisement for a soda brand that focused on the ingredients. It may not be possible. Marketing is about selling a feeling, or an aspiration. It is essential to build a relationship with your customer. If you limit your product descriptions to the physical attributes of your products, you are missing a great opportunity to create a connection with potential customers.

What makes them better than the other items similar to them?

Even though the products on Etsy are handmade, customized, and not manufactured in a factory for mass production, there is still a chance that your items are not the only one of their kind on the site. Chances are, you are not the only one who makes and sells such items. For example, if you are selling knitted clothing, you can expect other sellers to sell knitted clothing as well. It is actually pretty common to sell knitted sweaters and other clothes, so you need to make sure that your products have something that can make them stand out from the rest. So, how can you make your products distinguished? Well, you can demonstrate and explain the competitive advantage of your products. What is it that makes your items better than other similar items? What quality and characteristic does your product have? See to it that you elevate your merchandise by demonstrating their unique features, but be careful not to bash the other sellers. You can also explain the way your products can help make the lives of your customers easier, more fun, or more convenient.

What is the cost of your merchandise?

In Etsy, the cost is practically a given. However, if you are trying to pin your crafts or blog, you may tend to overlook the price. Do not be shy because the prices of your products should not be a detriment to shoppers if you have done the necessary research.

What is the size of your item?

It can be difficult to determine the size of items when they are isolated. This is why you have to provide your customers with a sense of scale. You can do this by taking photos of your items with you or a model. You can also place it beside a pet or another familiar object. For example, if you are selling handmade dolls, your customers may not know how small or big they are unless they see it with something they already know the size of. So if you are selling this doll and it is only as big as the palm of your hand, you can put it on your palm and take its picture. This would give your customers a better idea of how big it is instead of just putting it down on the ground and taking a picture. If you are selling an artwork, you can hang it on your wall and take a picture. If you are selling a piece of jewelry, you can either hold it up or put it on. You can also put it on a mannequin. The same thing goes with clothing. You can either wear the clothes yourself or put it on a life size mannequin.

Image taken from etsy.com

◢ How many items are included?

The quantity is fairly obvious for most products. For others, however, you have to make it clear. You have to indicate how many pieces your buyers are going to receive once they pay for your merchandise. This is usually the case for craft supplies and greeting cards. The same thing goes for handmade envelopes and other kinds of stationery.

◢ How does your item fit?

This is highly crucial for items that are meant to be worn. Shirts, blouses, pants, and skirts should include measurements. Socks, hats, and accessories may be photographed on a model or mannequin. You have to show the items on a mannequin or model to show them on a scale. Otherwise, it would be difficult to determine whether they are too small or too big for the wearer. The main objective is to let your customers know how the item would fit them.

Image taken from theshopcompany.com

◢ How is the item used?

You must always include an action shot or two. This is especially true if your merchandise is meant to be used with another item. For instance, if you are selling an iPad stand, you have to show your item holding up an actual iPad. If you are selling a cellphone case, you have to show it with a cellphone. If you are selling custom passport holders, you have to have an actual passport featuring the passport holder. What if your item is a downloadable one? Let us say that you are selling downloadable recipe books. You can show potential customers your recipe by cooking a dish and showing the recipe beside it. This way, your potential customers will get an idea of how the finished dish will look like and what they can expect when they purchase and download your virtual recipe book.

Image taken from www.etsy.com

What are the available options?

As much as possible, you have to show every available option. This way, your customers can maximize their choices. If possible, you should also include a chart to keep things organized. For example, if you are selling personalized notebooks and they come in different colors, you should inform your customers about the available colors. If you are selling bespoke items, you should inform your customers about the parts that are customizable.

What are your products made of?

It is important to tell your customers about the materials that you used in making your products. By doing so, you give them an idea about the quality and sturdiness of such products. For example, if you are selling furniture, such as tables and chairs, you should tell them if you used wood, metal, or a combination of both. If you used wood, you should tell which what kind of wood you used. As you know, the different types of wood also have different levels of strength. Some types are sturdier and tend to last longer than the others. You should also inform them about the finish and other processes you used in making the item. If you are selling clothes, you should include the components you used in the description. This should include the fabric, dyes, stains, zippers, buttons, etc. Most customers who browse Etsy are also in search of natural products. So if you are selling modeling clays, face masks, lotions, soaps, and other similar products, see to it that you mention in your description if they are organic, hypoallergenic, gluten-free, or low in volatile organic compounds (VOC's).

Is your merchandise, pre-made, a pattern, or custom order?

Unfortunately, so many customers tend to mistake these three. However, they are all different, which is why you have to make sure that you are clear when you discuss them in your descriptions. Obviously, 'pre-made' or 'already made' is a finished product; 'custom order' is something that a customer requests to be done or something that is bespoke; while a 'pattern' is a raw product or practically a guide that the customers need to come up with the finished product themselves. Why do you need to indicate if it is any of these three? Sometimes, sellers post photos of products even if they are not all pre-made. For example, instead of posting a photo of the pattern, they post the finished product that used the pattern. If you are selling custom order items or patterns, your customers might think that they would be paying for the exact items in your photos. So in order to avoid confusion and misunderstanding, indicate in your description if the item is pre-made, a pattern, or custom order.

Chapter 11: How to Determine Pricing

Pricing is another one of the most crucial aspects that you have to know about as a seller. In the competitive world of Etsy, you have to set prices that are competitive as well. You do not want to set them too high because they will not be so appealing to the masses. At the same time, you do not want to set them too low because it might cause potential customers to speculate about the quality of your items.

There are people who do not mind spending hours just to browse and research for the perfect bag or necklace. Others, however, are more interested in finding high quality items. Nevertheless, regardless of their preferences, there is basically one thing that nearly every purchasing decision has in common: the price.

If it is too pricey, people might say that it is impractical and look somewhere else. If it is too inexpensive, they might think that it is not made of good quality materials. You have to set a price that is just right in order for you to make a profit and keep on encouraging potential customers to make a purchase. Keep in mind that a healthy profit margin is necessary if you want to keep your business running.

How to Set the Right Price

For starters, you can create a worksheet that will help you evaluate your expenses. To help you determine a good price, you have to consider factors, such as time, material costs, overhead expenses, and labor. Begin by filling in the numbers on your worksheet depending on how much you currently spend. Afterwards, consider what you may modify in order to improve the bottom line.

You can start with the materials involved in making your product. Jot down every material you used along with their respective prices. If you are selling craft supplies or vintage items, see to it that you input their costs when you bought them. You can experiment by deleting a material to find out how that alters the costs. Then, you should observe what happens when you reduce the material cost. If you can buy supplies in bulk, how do you think would that affect your costs?

Next, you should take overhead into account. Create a list of the business expenses that are not related to specific items. For instance, if you are renting a studio space, paying for gas when you go to the supply store, or buying equipment necessary for your business, you have to take those factors into consideration too. See to it that you keep these costs documented. Afterwards, divide them according to how many items you currently have in stock or plan to produce within the year.

Taking these things into consideration lets you have a rough estimate of how much price to set. This is a good way on how you have an estimated overhead cost for every item. In addition, you can experiment by changing the number of items you produce every year or deleting any overhead expenditure you can do without.

Do not forget to cover labor. As you know, it takes some time to finish producing, packaging, and shipping items. You should consider the production process per task. Overall, you should determine how many hours it takes to prepare your product for sale. Also, you should know what you have to pay yourself for everything that you do. Figure out how much you would have made if you were working a day job.

If you are the only one who does all the work, then you have to give yourself more credit. Production, shipping, handling, packaging, answering e-mails, and editing photos are not easy to do. Even if you are having fun running your business, you should still make sure that you pay yourself. You can do an experiment by eliminating a certain task or decreasing the time a single step takes. You can also try different hourly wages. Moreover, you can consider being more efficient by doing two tasks at once or maybe even paying yourself more.

You have to make pricing one of your goals. However, you have to be realistic. If your business has just started, being able to break even can already be an accomplishment. If you think that you are ready to venture into wholesale, then you may want to reevaluate your pricing structure. Make sure that you consider the scope of your shop as well as where you want to be by the end of the year. When you price for the present, do not forget to price for the future as well.

How to Test If the Price Is Right

When you have finally gotten a good picture of what you currently spend, you can start testing if the price is right. Keep in mind that just because you think your price is right does not mean that customers think the same way. Some of them may not be willing to pay the amount that you set. This is why you have to research and test your prices to see if they will 'click' with customers.

To help you calculate the right price, you have to do research and testing. Find out how much you would ideally spend on every part of the process in order for you to reach such pricing goal. The following steps can help you figure out what an ideal price should look like:

1. **Research**. See to it that you consider the position of your prices in the ecosystem of online selling platforms, such as Etsy. Consider how your prices compare to others. Keep in mind that the things sold in huge stores do not usually have the additional value of personally made, unique pieces. Hence, they are not really your direct competitors, although you can use their prices as references.
2. **Determine your target audience**. See to it that you get a clear picture of which types of people you want to market your items to. Also, make sure that you consider the occasion when they are most likely to purchase your merchandise. For instance, if you are selling maps, your materials are cheap since they are just mostly paper and ink. However, since your target audience consists mostly of people in search of unique gifts for their family

and friends during special occasions such as birthdays and holidays, you should not hesitate to charge a higher price.

3. **Test and gauge the response of other people**. Once you have decided on a final price, see to it that you obtain feedback from other people, such as customers and fellow sellers. Feel free to ask questions that may be helpful for your business. Talk to the people in your own network as well as seek advice via the Etsy Teams. Furthermore, you can do the A/B test, which is a process that involves setting different prices for similar items in order to find out how well they can sell.

How to Meet In the Middle

If you think about it, using the approaches stated above can yield different results. Do not worry if you happen to have slightly varying results because you can use that as an opportunity to find out why that happened. You should use your worksheet to identify which levers you have to pull as well as how to make the necessary adjustments for your business.

Figure out if you have to use fewer or less expensive raw materials or if you have to eliminate some tasks and boost your efficiency. Ponder if continuing certain details is still worth your time. If they are very labor intensive, then you may consider quitting them. Always keep in mind that your prices are basically a continuous work in progress. You should never stop reevaluating your approach whenever you spot a change in the business ecosystem or your shop.

Is There a Formula You Can Use to Price Your Items?

Yes, there is. However, there is no single formula for this. You can tweak your formula depending on your circumstances. What works for other people may not exactly work for you. Nevertheless, this chapter will discuss a generic pricing formula that you can use for your Etsy shop. You can use this formula:

materials + expenses + labor + profit = 2 (wholesale) = retail

As you can see, the formula lets you properly account for your profit. Let us discussed the elements involved in the above mentioned formula.

Materials

It is crucial for you to take your materials into consideration. See to it that all your material fees are covered. After all, it is pretty common for sellers to neglect certain things such as the costs of thread and packaging. Remember that every little thing counts!

Expenses

What are the expenses involved in the production of your items? Perhaps, you had to buy an e-book or watch tutorials for hours just so you can learn how to make your product. Maybe you had to rent a studio and drive or commute to it every day to manage your business. All of these factors are crucial in maintaining your business and making it grow. Thus, you have to take them into consideration. But how can you fit all of them into a single price?

Again, writing down or creating a worksheet for your expenses is necessary. Everything that is involved in the production of your items should be included in the list. Then, you should determine how many items you plan to sell per month, and divide this number into your overall expenses.

If you want to obtain a more exact price, you should carefully track your expenses by using an accounting tool. You can purchase a software program or use a free version online. Also, make sure that you figure out your huge investments. For instance, if you bought a sewing machine, you have to figure out how many garments you can sew with it. If you ordered a postage printer, you should find out how long it can last before you have to replace it.

Labor

You should compare yourself and the work you do to others who are in the same field. This way, you can have a good estimate of how much you should pay yourself. For instance, if you are in the business of making and selling clothes, you should research and find out how much dressmakers and tailors make in your area. Since you are most probably designing the clothes as well, you also have to find out how much clothing designers make. You may even be the accountant, administrative assistant, marketing department, and janitor too. Do not hesitate to pay yourself more if you think you deserve it.

Profit

You have to consider where you want your business to be in the long run. If you are planning to quit your day job or you have to pay off your student loans, then you really have to account for your profit. However, this can depend on what you are marketing and selling. So, make sure that you consider all factors involved.

Wholesale

There are sellers who wonder if they can use wholesale prices in their shops. If you are planning to sell your work at these prices, you should stop right there. Selling at wholesale prices is not a good way to sell your work at affordable prices. Instead, you have to make your wholesale price double and sell your merchandise at a retail price.

First of all, when you sell your items at a wholesale price, you undervalue the people who price their items at the right retail prices. This happens whether or not you intend it to. Keep in mind that if you price your work thoughtfully, everyone who sells items in the same category will benefit.

Second, your customers may start wondering why you are pricing your work so lowly. They would start to question why your work is much lower than the others. This may lead them to think that your items are not really handmade or that they are made from cheap materials.

Finally, you put yourself at a disadvantage when you sell at wholesale prices. Just think of it, what if a huge catalog contacts you and tells you that they want to purchase hundreds of your items and they want to know how much you charge for wholesale? If you are selling at low prices, you might miss out on making a huge profit.

Chapter 12: Utilizing SEO

Search engine optimization or SEO is one of the most important elements of online marketing. So if you are trying to sell online, you have to make use of it properly. A lot of sellers on Etsy tend to struggle when it comes to getting found in the search engines. This is most likely the result of poor search engine optimization. In order for you to avoid making the same mistakes, see to it that you adhere to the following guidelines:

◢ Brainstorm key phrases and keywords.

Keep in mind that every listing has to begin with a list of key phrases and keywords that your target audience is most likely to use when they browse online. Make sure that you use this list. Also, make sure that your tags, titles, and descriptions all answer the questions that customers are most likely to ask. Moreover, do not hesitate to use the search bar so you can keep track of what customers usually search for. Just type in your items in the search bar and you will see which words are popular amongst customers. You can use this to have an idea of what customers like, want, and need. Incorporate these key phrases and keywords to your tags, titles, and descriptions if they are relevant. You can also use synonymous words.

Work your search terms into your listings.

Once you finalize your list of key phrases and keywords, you should start working them into your listings. Make your titles powerful. Keep them customer-friendly and enticing, but do not forget to add terms that may be meaningful to shoppers. You should also keep your most crucial search terms at the start of the listing in order to make the most of their importance in the search engines.

Take note that just because you included the main category in the title does not mean that your relevancy in the search engines will improve. Nevertheless, doing so allows you to inform your customers what your items are. You can try experimenting by incorporating certain words in your titles that might turn shop browsers into actual paying customers.

See to it that you also make the most of your tags. As much as possible, you should use every available space and plug in all key phrases and keywords. Remember that every one of these words can help you find another potential customer.

Moreover, take note that diversity is important. It is not a good idea to group similar items and use the same name for them. If you do this, you will only reach out to a single type of customer. In order for you to gain more attention, you have to be diverse in using key phrases and keywords. Do your best to target different types of customers through search results.

You should place the most important terms in your tags and titles. If your titles are quite long, you can place the most important search terms at the beginning so that they can be in the first line.

Be accurate when categorizing your items.

As a seller, reviewing categories is absolutely a must. Remember that when customers use the search filters, they see items according to their categories. So, you should think of the places customers are most likely to look into when you categorize your items. You can use individual listings, for instance. You can also use bulk category editing in the Listings Manager option.

Monitor your statistics.

See to it that you monitor the statistics of your shop to find out if your strategies are really working. Your shop stats tells you which keywords and key phrases people usually use when they look for you. Use the information you acquired to help you improve your tags, titles, and descriptions. Do not hesitate to use listed words that you have not used yet. You can also use synonyms with the popular key phrases and keywords.

What if you get a lot of hits but do not make a lot of sales? Well, this may happen if you optimize incorrect key phrases and keywords. So, be sure to test out new key phrases and keywords to see which ones work. See to it that you also become more specific with your style. If the situation calls for it, you have to be ready to make chances. Nonetheless, if your search items already bring customers to your shop, then you can make huge changes gradually so you can find out which strategies are working perfectly fine before you strategize some more.

Encourage clicks.

Etsy has a search algorithm that takes into consideration how well items do in search. This is called the listing quality, and it is meant to show which items customers are likely to buy. Each time a customer buys, clicks, or "favorites" an item they found in the search results, they contribute to the quality score of that particular listing. If you wish to improve the quality of your listing, you should have more interaction with your customers. You can upload photos of your products and encourage customers to click on them for a clearer closeup view.

Guarantee customer satisfaction.

Nobody wants to have an unpleasant experience when buying from a shop. Hence, you should make an effort to let your customers know that they will surely have a wonderful time at your shop. Check to see if your shipping profiles are completed, so you can represent the processing time accurately to your customers. Make sure that you also tell a good story. As you have learned in the previous chapters, a story that inspires, motivates, and touches the heart can help you gain more customers.

Bring it all together.

Do not be afraid to seek help if you need it. If you ever find yourself struggling to improve your ranking in the search engines or come up with key phrases and keywords, you can ask other people to help you out. You can find support and encouragement in forums with regard to search engine optimization and relevancy.

Additional Pointers for Using Search Engine Optimization (SEO)

Now that you have learned about the importance of search engine optimization or SEO for your business, you may want to follow these tips to help you learn more about Etsy search engine optimization:

- **Make your first three words count, and then repeat.**

  Keep in mind that the first three words you use for your title are the most crucial for search engine optimization. While the entirety of your title is important, it is the first three words that capture the attention of the reader. Also, they tend to be the closest reflection of your item. So in order for you to be able to make the most of Etsy SEO, you should use the first three words in your title twice – one in the first sentence of the description of your item and another one in its tag. Then, you should use keyword phrases in your tags and titles.

  For instance, if you have a listing entitled "Pink Panther Bracelet – Limited Edition for Fall Cat Collection", you can begin your description with "This pink panther bracelet is a fall season limited edition… " You should repeat your first three words so they can be ingrained in the minds of your customers and convince them to make a purchase. However, you should be careful not to force the words into the sentence. Do your best to sound as natural as you can.

- **Use different titles.**

  If you use similar titles in your listings, you will not do well with Google. You see, the search engine does not like it when there is too much repetition. Thus, you should use different titles every time, even if your items are closely related or similar with one another. You can build good search engine optimization when you tweak the titles of your items. Do not forget to use keywords that reflect your items. Refrain from using random terms just to be found.

- **Use proper punctuation and spacing.**

After you exert effort in creating excellent titles, see to it that you use

the right punctuations. Take note that it is ideal to put a space before and after a dash. You can also use commas. You can contact Etsy or view their Help page to find out which symbols you can use in your titles. See to it that you do not use four or more words all written in uppercase letters in your titles. Also, make sure that you do not go beyond one hundred and forty characters. It is possible to get a preview of your titles, so do not hesitate to check out how they will appear on the search engines.

Use all tag spaces.

Think of your tags as pathways to your Etsy shop. If you leave one of them blank, you would miss a pathway and a potential customer. This is why you have to make sure that everything is filled, including *Categories*. Your categories are practically your first three tags. Thus, see to it that you choose wisely. Overall, every one of your items gets to have sixteen spaces for tags. These include the three categories and their thirteen subcategories.

Consider the holidays and recent trends.

When you choose your keyword tags, do not forget to consider the holidays and the recent trends. Using holiday tags is a great way to increase your views as well as your chances of being featured on the Etsy blog or front page. Etsy actually promotes holidays in the Browse category on their front page. They also periodically release blog posts that feature the recent trends, popular colors, and holiday themes.

Consider other countries.

Remember that Etsy is known globally, so you should not focus on just one country, unless you purposely want to limit your demographics. If you want to reach out to customers abroad, see to it that you consider their countries. For instance, you should use alternate spellings and foreign translations. You should also consider the holidays that   they are celebrating in their country, so you can produce items that are fitting for such occasions.

Chapter 13: Tips on Selling Vintage Items

Etsy is known to be an online marketplace for handmade items. However, as you have learned, the site has started to allow sellers to offer vintage items, provided that these items are at least twenty years old. If you are an enthusiast for vintage items and would like to sell them in your Etsy shop, here are some tips that could help you out:

Use good and appropriate tags.

You have already learned how you can use tags to improve your search engine optimization. Then again, tags are not only useful for SEO purposes. In fact, they can also increase your chances of making a sale. Try to think in the perspective of the buyer instead of the seller. What do you think buyers want to see when they search for vintage items on Etsy? For example, if you are selling a vintage globe, you should consider its type, appearance, and other related elements. Use the most ideal keywords and key phrases, not just generic ones. The keywords "globe" and "blue" may be too generic and boring. Be specific with your tags as much as possible. So instead of using just "globe" and "blue", you can indicate the name of the manufacturer and the year the globe was made in your keywords.

Upload good photos.

Again, the importance of uploading good photos cannot be stressed enough. A picture can really paint a thousand words. So if you want people to see how amazing your item is, you have to capture its essence in photos. While using vintage effects for your vintage item photos may seem appealing, it is highly inappropriate for your Etsy shop. As a seller, you have to be credible. You have to show your customers the actual look of your product, along with its dents, scratches, stains, etc. Do not try to conceal flaws because these flaws are actually good. They contribute more to the authenticity of the item. So if the vintage item has an engraving, embroidered name, or visible mark on it, just let it be and include it in the photo.

Image taken from www.shutterstock.com

Market and promote your items.

It is pretty inexpensive to sell on Etsy. However, the marketing and promoting aspects of selling are all on you. You can have a shop on Etsy, but if you do not have an outlet to market and promote your items, you will not be able to make lots of profit. So, make sure that you use every possible outlet there is. You can use social networking sites, blogs, and forums. Broaden your network as much as possible, so you can reach out to more people. Since you are selling vintage items, you can also check out sites where antique owners and enthusiasts gather to discuss their collections, and inform them of your items. Antique and vintage pieces are loved by people of different ages and walks of life. Surely, there is someone out there who would be willing to purchase your vintage item.

Include the history of the items.

Everybody loves a good story. You have learned how including a good story in your description can make a huge impact on the decision of customers to make a purchase. If you are selling a vintage purse, for example, you can tell potential customers about its origins and previous owner. Tell them how you got the item, who its previous owner was, where the previous owner lived, where the purse was manufactured, etc. The more interesting the story is, the higher the likelihood that the item will be purchased. In addition, if your item is tied to a famous person, such as a celebrity, politician, or inventor, you can charge a higher price. Collectors love to purchase items that are once owned by famous people and would typically do and pay for anything just to get them.

Indicate the current condition of the item.

It is your responsibility as a seller to inform your customers of the current state of the vintage item. Is it still in good condition or is it starting to wear out? Is it still working or is it just good for being displayed on the shelf? For example, if you are selling old books, you should inform potential customers about the pages and the covers. Are some pages torn or missing? Are there writings on the cover? If you are a comic book collector and would like to sell some of your collections, be sure to include if the items are in mint condition. If you are selling a non-working antique telephone, you should tell your customers that the item does not function anymore. Do not forget to give them instructions on how to handle the items to prevent damage.

Image taken from www.shutterstock.com

Made in the USA
Middletown, DE
13 December 2022

18293972R00045